Bordeaux
Travel Guide

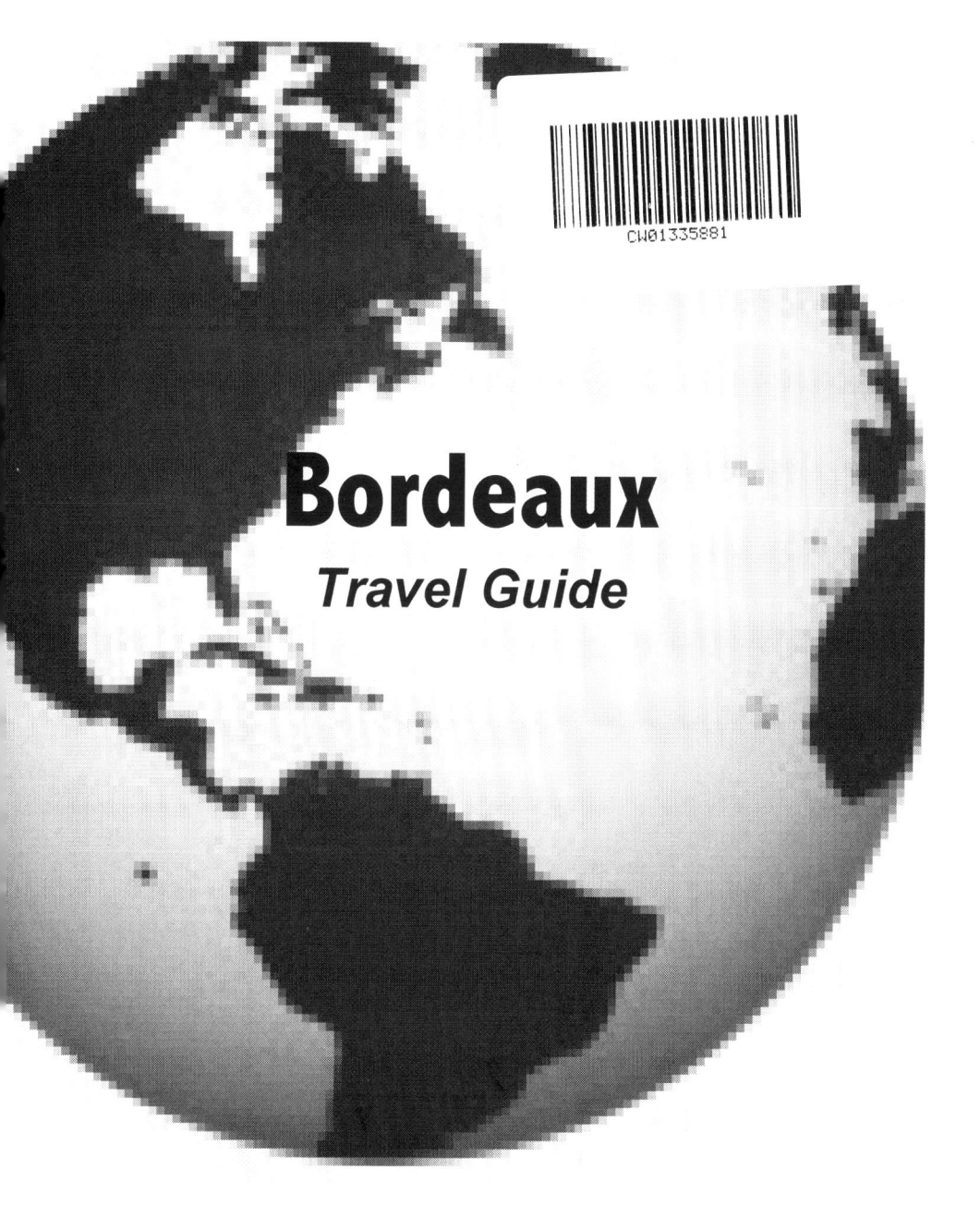

Quick Trips Series

No part of this publication may be reproduced, stored in a retrieval system, or transmitted, in any form or by any means without the prior written permission of the publisher, nor be otherwise circulated in any form of binding or cover other than that in which it is published and without similar condition being imposed on the subsequent purchaser. If there are any errors or omissions in copyright acknowledgements the publisher will be pleased to insert the appropriate acknowledgement in any subsequent printing of this publication. Although we have taken all reasonable care in researching this book we make no warranty about the accuracy or completeness of its content and disclaim all liability arising from its use.

Copyright © 2016, Astute Press
All Rights Reserved.

Table of Contents

BORDEAUX & THE WINE REGION — 5
- Customs & Culture 6
- Geography 8
- Weather & Best Time to Visit 9

SIGHTS & ACTIVITIES: WHAT TO SEE & DO — 10
- Bordeaux Wine Regions 10
  - The Médoc Region 14
  - The Graves Region 15
  - The Right Bank 17
  - Saint Émilion 18
- Museum of Wines 20
- Bordeaux 21
  - Churches of Bordeaux 22
  - Jardin Botanique de Bordeaux 23
  - Parc Majorlan, Blanquefort 23
- Château de la Brède 24
- Prehistoric Sites 25
- Bay of Arcachon 26
  - Dune du Pyla 26
  - Arcachon Museum & Aquarium 27
- Accommodation 28

Ibis Bordeaux Centre Bastide 28
Hotel Gambetta 29
Hotel Le Chantry 29
Chez Simon 30
Staying at a Wine Chateau 30

◉ Places to Eat 32
Le Parlement des Graves 32
Vinset 33
Lard et Bouchon 34
Le Petit Port 34
Chai Pascal 35

◉ Shopping 35
How To Buy Affordable Wine in Bordeaux 35
Cadiot-Badie 37
Les Douceurs de Louise 37
Rue Saint Catherine 38
La Mauvaise Réputation 38

KNOW BEFORE YOU GO — 40

◉ Entry Requirements 40
◉ Health Insurance 41
◉ Travelling with Pets 41
◉ Airports 42
◉ Airlines 44
◉ Currency 45
◉ Banking & ATMs 45
◉ Credit Cards 45
◉ Tourist Taxes 46
◉ Reclaiming VAT 46
◉ Tipping Policy 47
◉ Mobile Phones 47

- 🌐 **Dialling Code** 48
- 🌐 **Emergency Numbers** 48
- 🌐 **Time Zone** 49
- 🌐 **Daylight Savings Time** 50
- 🌐 **School Holidays** 50
- 🌐 **Driving Laws** 50
- 🌐 **Drinking Laws** 51
- 🌐 **Smoking Laws** 52
- 🌐 **Electricity** 52
- 🌐 **Food & Drink** 53

BORDEAUX TRAVEL GUIDE

Bordeaux & the Wine Region

The French wine region of Bordeaux evokes a rich sensory experience with many. Prepare to experience the regions rich red wines, inhale their rich bouquets and experience the aromas with their seductive refinement. There is, however, more to Bordeaux than just vineyards. At the heart of the region, lies its capital. Bordeaux can be called a city that wine built and it reflects the elegant and exquisitely beautiful inheritance of wine through its art, its architecture and its love of the good things in life.

There is a touch of eternity to Bordeaux's reputation. The Romans introduced winemaking to the region and, two thousand years later, long after the might of Rome has fallen, Bordeaux continues to make wine.

It saw Bacchus, god of the vine make way for the earliest ambassadors of the Christian era. It embraced a merry union with Old England, when its First Daughter, Eleanor of Aquitaine married Henry II of England in the romantic era of the medieval troubadours. It saw its produce shipped to New Worlds, to be traded for small fortunes. Through all the changes of the outside world, season after season, grapes are grown and harvested, for a next vintage.

The excellent wines of Bordeaux have exerted an important influence of the development of a matching tradition of culinary excellence. The enjoyment of food is taken very seriously, and here, the challenge is not only to delight the palate, but, more importantly, to successfully pair a good wine to its compliment in the form of a tasty meal.

Customs & Culture

Cave paintings and fossil evidence suggest that parts of the region of Bordeaux had been settled since prehistoric times. The original inhabitants, Aquitani are believed to have been Indo-Europeans, distantly related to the Basques. The Romans first colonized the area around 56 BC and are credited with introducing the first vineyards to the region.

During the early middle ages, it came to be included in Charlemagne's Frankish empire, although the area later gained autonomy as the Duchy of Aquitaine. With the marriage of Eleanor of Aquitaine to Henry II of England in 1154, the region came to be an English possession, which it remained, until the conclusion of the Hundred Year War in the 15th century, when it reverted to French rule. It was during this time, that French

BORDEAUX TRAVEL GUIDE

wines, particularly clarets, became sought after in England. In the 16th and 17th century, the area became an important bastion of France's beleaguered Protestant minority, the Huguenots.

Today the population of Bordeaux is mainly Catholic, but includes Protestants and Muslims. The region is known for its tolerance towards minorities and alternative lifestyles. As the region's capital includes the campus of Bordeaux University, the city has a lively, vibrant atmosphere one might associate with a large student population. Despite its many Gothic inspired buildings, there is a willingness to experiment with creativity. This is expressed in the Modern Art bus, established to search after new and exciting forms of visual art and the Barbey School of Rock, a fun alternative to classic musical training that regularly organizes concerts and other outside activities.

People from Bordeaux are referred to as "Bordelais" and the pace of life is leisurely and easy-going. An annual wine festival with events scheduled at locations across the region, occurs in June or July. Although its capital is the hub of business and culture, the majority of the region remains refreshingly rural.

BORDEAUX TRAVEL GUIDE

🌐 Geography

Bordeaux is located on the southwestern part of France, near the Atlantic Ocean, falling within the region that was once known as the kingdom of Aquitaine. The Gironde Estuary and its two great tributaries, the Dordogne and the Garonne, bisect the area. Nearly all the wine-growing areas are arranged around the banks of the banks of these rivers and some of the area, such as much of Medoc, was originally reclaimed from swampland.

Bordeaux divides into four sub-regions. Of these, Médoc and Graves are located along the Left Bank of the Gironde River. The Right Bank is made up of the Libournais, Bourg and Blaye. There are a number of further distinctions. Médoc, the most prestigious of the group, can further be divided into the upstream part in the south, which also goes by the name of Haut-Médoc and the downriver portion in the north, sometimes referred to as Bas-Médoc, but often simply known as Médoc. Each sub-region represents a number of appellations. The term appellation is used to describe the strict production and quality standards that define the wine that originates from a specific area. An appellation would in turn function as a commune representing various wine producers or chateaus within a distinct area.

BORDEAUX TRAVEL GUIDE

At the heart of the region, lies its capital, the city of Bordeaux. It occupies a curve along the Garonne River, which is at that point still accessible to large ships such as ocean liners. As the fourth largest city in France, it is serviced by its own airport, but also has a port large enough to offer access to oceanic liners. Through the Eurolines bus service, it is connected to destinations throughout Europe such as Madrid, Oslo, Prague, Amsterdam, Milan, and even Gdansk.

There are various ways to getting out and about in Bordeaux. The region has an affordable and reliable bus and train network. If you are planning to travel around the wine district, you may wish to explore the options of independent transport. Young and energetic visitors may have no qualms about cycling through the vineyards. A less labour-intensive option is to organize a car, either by rental or, if you are planning to stay a little longer, through the Eurodrive programme, which allows temporary ownership of a brand new Renault, with a guaranteed buy-back option, vehicle insurance and a reliable GPS system.

🌍 Weather & Best Time to Visit

Bordeaux enjoys a coastal climate with warm, dry summers and cool, wet winters. The region sees an average rainfall of 900mm per year, with the wettest month typically being December. A fair amount of rain also falls in the spring and autumn months. Snow, sleet and hail sometimes occur in January and February.

From June to September, day temperatures in the low to mid twenties can be expected. July and August are the warmest months with average highs of 25 and 26 degrees Celsius respectively. Night temperatures of around 12 to 14 degrees Celsius are recorded for those months. By contrast, the coldest months are December and January, when day temperatures seldom rise above 9 degrees Celsius and night temperatures of around 2 to 3 degrees Celsius can be expected. The early part of spring still sees day averages between 15 and 17 degrees Celsius, but in May, daily highs show a slight rise to reach 20 degrees Celsius. Temperatures between 8 and 18 degrees Celsius can be expected for October, while November usually records a cool 5 to 13 degrees Celsius.

Sights & Activities: What to See & Do

🌍 Bordeaux Wine Regions

Bordeaux is widely acknowledged as the most famous wine region in France, accounting for well over 10,000 wine producers and an annual output of around 850 million bottles of wine. Rare vintages from the region have been known to fetch record prices at auctions, such as a 6-litre bottle of 1947 Cheval

BORDEAUX TRAVEL GUIDE

Blanc from Bordeaux which sold for $304,000 at Christies in New York.

The wines of Bordeaux are classified according to a hierarchy first defined in 1855, in response to an invitation from Napoleon III to participate in the Great Exposition of the same year. According to this ranking system, which is still used today, the produce of 58 chateaux were divided into five groups, based on their quality. The most prestigious rank is that of First Growths, which is given only to wines that represent a tradition of excellence dating back hundreds of years. These are the wines that consistently retail at around $1000 per bottle today. Only five wines carry this distinction, and of these, three

BORDEAUX TRAVEL GUIDE

are found in the Pauillac appellation in the prestigious Médoc sub-region.

A number of aspects contribute towards the region's suitability as wine land. The proximity of the Atlantic Ocean moderates the climate, cooling off the region in summer and preventing the occurrence of frost in winter. The soil ranges in diversity from gravel from the Pyrenees to limestone and clay. A term you will probably encounter frequently within the wine land is terroir. This refers to the way elements in the soil of a particular chateau or wine producer express themselves in the aroma of the grapes grown and ultimately the wine produced from them. In the Bordeaux region, this can be as individual as a signature.

The most common grapes planted are red varieties, and of these, Merlot grapes account for fifty percent of all Bordeaux vineyards. Other red grapes types of the region include Cabernet Sauvignon, Cabernet Franc, Petit Verdot, Malbec and Carmenere. White grape types include Sémillon, Sauvignon Blanc, Muscadelle, Ungi Blanc, Colombard and Folle Blanche. A long tradition of wine making has led to sub-regions being defined as appellations and optimized to produce a certain type of wine. Strict rules regarding grape varieties, winemaking methods, alcohol content and storage have to be adhered to. There are around sixty different appellations in the Bordeaux

BORDEAUX TRAVEL GUIDE

region. The most famous of these are St Emillion, Pauilllac, St Estephe and St Julien.

The wine industry of Bordeaux is close to 2000 years old, but wine tourism is an invention of recent vintage in the region. There are a number of packages available that offer one day, two day or even three-day excursions into the vineyards of Bordeaux. A day excursion which includes pickup at your hotel, visits to three wine chateaux's plus lunch can be expected to cost anywhere between €55 and €390. If you wish to compile an independent itinerary, bear in mind that you would probably spend 90 minutes to two hours per wine estate. It is also best to let the establishment know in advance of your plans.

Although the famous four may seem inaccessible, it is possible to book a tour independently, with a little advance planning. Free tours can be booked at Chateaux Latour via email at s.guerlou@chateau-latour.com, provided that you approach them at least four weeks in advance. Chateaux Latife Rothschild need at least five weeks notice, for the arrangement of a one-hour tour in English or French. Email them at visites@lafite.com to book. Chateaux Margaux also requires five weeks notice and can be approached through their website at http://www.chateau-margaux.com/en/.

BORDEAUX TRAVEL GUIDE

The Médoc Region

The Médoc is well known for the classic reds it cultivates. The region can be found along the left bank of the Gironde River, stretching from the mouth of the river to the city of Bordeaux. It is the home of some of the most famous wine appellations, such as St-Estephe, Pauillac, St. Julien and Margaux.

One of the most sought after appellations in the Haut-Medoc region has to be Pauillac. Located between Saint-Estephe and Saint Julien, it is widely known for the superior quality of its red wines. Two of the original top five, namely Chateaux Latour and Latife Rothschild, belongs to this appellation and a later addition, Chateau Mouton-Rothschild, can also be found here. The wines of Pauillac are described as full-bodied, tannic and acid when young, but expressing aromas of cedar and blackcurrent with proper aging. Pauillac represents 115 separate vine growers, who produce 8.5 million bottles annually.

By comparison, Saint-Julien is a modest appellation, but it produces powerful red wines with a strong aroma, that mature well. The commune of Saint-Julien includes the villages, Beychevelle and Saint-Julien-Beychevelle. The appellation of Saint-Estephe represents a variety of soil types that include clay, gravel and sand and the wines it produces, are similarly unusual and distinct. They are full-bodied, but mature a little slower than the other wines of the Medoc and make great purchases to enhance the contents of your wine cellar. The soil of the Margaux appellation is composed of deposits of mountainous gravel. Here a medium to full-bodied red wine with a unique and delicate bouquet is produced. The prize achievement of the commune is Château Margaux, an estate that dates back to the 12th century and was once the location of a fortified castle called Lamothe. Its vineyard of 100 hectares produces around 300,000 bottles per year.

There are several museums in the Medoc region worth visiting. Château Mouton-Rothschild, in the Pauillac commune has a museum dedicated to art related to the wine making process. It exhibits a variety of tapestries and paintings. The museum at Château Loudenne in Saint Yzans de Médoc focuses on the tools and instruments used in winemaking. Vinorama at 12 cours du Medoc showcases the history of Bordeaux wines, dating back to the time of the Romans and Château Maucaillou in Moulis en Médoc features a museum that centers around a historical wine cellar from 1875.

The Graves Region

Like Médoc, Graves is located along the left bank of the Gironde River, southeast of the city Bordeaux. It enjoys a number of distinctions. Graves is widely considered to be the

BORDEAUX TRAVEL GUIDE

original birthplace of claret, and also the first beneficiary of the wine trade between Bordeaux and England. Château Pape Clément, planted in the year 1300, lays claim to being the oldest château of the region and the first to bear an official name. The vineyard was gifted to Bertrand de Goth, who later became Pope Clément V. Château Pape Clément employs the influential wine consultant Michel Rolland. The Graves is also home to Château Haut-Brion, one of the original First Growths listed in the Bordeaux Wine Official Classification of 1855. In the past few centuries, it has lost some of its prestige to its left bank neighbor, Médoc.

While the main Graves appellation is known for dry reds blended mainly from Cabernet Sauvignon and Merlot, but with hints of Cabernet Franc, Petit Verdot and Malbec, the region of the Graves has a few smaller appellations, that favor semi-sweet white wines.

BORDEAUX TRAVEL GUIDE

The Right Bank

Blaye is located on the Right Bank and represented several appellations such as Blaye AOC, Cotes de Blaye AOC and Premiers Cotes de Blaye AOC. These were updated in 1990 and according to the new specifications, Blaye AOC produces exclusively reds, while Cotes de Blaye AOC produces exclusively whites. Further restructuring led to one unifying appellation, Cotes de Bordeaux Blaye. In this region, the terrain is hillier and the soil is closer to clay, ideal territory for growing Merlot grapes. Blaye is known for its fruity wines that are best enjoyed while still fairly young.

Libourne, historically known as Leybornia, can be found where the Isle joins the Dordogne River, about 8 km from St Emilion. During the late Middle Ages, the region saw heavy fighting between the English and the French over the possession of Gironde. The town has a number of interesting historical features. There is a Gothic church and a clock tower dating back to the 14th century that once formed part of the town's fortification. The town house dates back to the 16th century. There is also a monument dedicated to Elie, duc Decazes, a prime minister of France from the 19th century. Besides good wine, the area is known for its culinary delights. The region includes one of the most legendary vineyards, that of Saint Emilion.

The Côtes de Bourg appellation is located on the right bank of the Dordogne, where it meets the Gironde. The first vineyards date back to the 2nd century AD, but the area was also mined extensively for tin and limestone. Its wines are described as medium-bodied and tannic with strong aromas of red fruit. It encloses the town Bourg-sur-Gironde and once functioned as a port for the export of its produce.

Saint Émilion

Although there is a lot of glamour attached to the Left Bank, one of the most significant appellations of Bordeaux is found on the right bank, in the Libournais region. Saint-Emilion was the

BORDEAUX TRAVEL GUIDE

first vineyard to be declared a UNESCO World Heritage site. The Romans planted its original vines in the 2nd century, but the location is named after Émilion, a monk from the eighth century. The area produces only red wines, that are known to be robust and full-bodied and produces approximately 36 million bottles a year.

Ecomusée du Libournais in Saint-Emilion is a museum centered on the history of different wine-makers. Some of the exhibits include reconstructions displaying old methods as well as a garden dedicated to instructing about the botanical aspects of growing vineyards. The institution also organizes hiking trips around the vines of the region. Contact them at Tel: +33 (0) 5 57 74 56 89 or via their website at http://www.ecomusee-libournais.com/.

There is another attraction of note in the region. The monolithic church of Saint Émilion was carved from a single block of limestone. There are four stained glass windows, as well as several tall pillars. If you are feeling energetic, you may wish to climb the 200 steps of the bell tower, which commands a great view of the area. One-hour tours are conducted in French and English. Admission is €7.

Bordering the Saint Émilion region is the Pomerol appellation. This is the home of Pétrus wine. Although recent by Bordeaux standards - the wine is first mentioned in 1837, Pétrus has rapidly risen in status to symbolize the allure of Bordeaux. It was served at the wedding off Prince Phillip to Queen Elizabeth and has appeared in numerous popular culture references. The estate itself is surprisingly modest, producing in a good year, no more than 2500 cases of wine. Pétrus produces exclusively red wines that are predominantly made of Merlot grapes.

🌐 Museum of Wines

41 Rue Borie, 33000 Bordeaux, France
Tel: +33 5 56 90 19 13

The building that houses the museum dates back to the 18th century and includes cellars from 1720. The museum documents the history of Bordeaux wine and also demonstrates how it is stored at the top end wine estates to preserve its quality. Attention is also given to the art of wine tasting and decanting. Exhibits include historical documents, bottles and other artefacts displaying the business of winemaking and wine trading. Admission is €7 and includes two wine tastings.

🌐 Bordeaux

The city of Bordeaux, alternately referred as the Port of the Moon and Sleeping Beauty, makes up one of the largest urban

BORDEAUX TRAVEL GUIDE

areas to be declared a UNESCO Heritage site. It has a number of interesting architectural features.

The Grand Theatre was designed by Victor Louis and completed in 1780. Its neo-Classical facade includes a portica of twelve Corinthian columns. These carry an entablature of twelve statues - the nine muses, joined by three goddesses, Juno, Venus and Minerva. It is home to the Opera National de Bordeaux and the Ballet National de Bordeaux.

A particularly memorable face of Bordeaux is the Place de la Bourse, and the unusual feature in front of it - a water mirror. The building was originally Place Royale and had been laid out by Jacques Gabriel on the instructions of Louis XV. Upon completion 1755, the centerpiece was an equestrian monument of the king. In the turbulent years following the French Revolution, the square was renamed several times until is became Place de la Bourse in 1848. The bronze statue of the king was dismantled and replaced by various other monuments. The self-replenishing water mirror, a recent addition, has transformed the area into a place where locals and visitors love to relax and perhaps engage in a little people watching. The Chamber of Commerce and the Customs Museum occupy the buildings on the square.

BORDEAUX TRAVEL GUIDE

Equally picturesque is Pont de Pierre, the first bridge to span the Garonne River. It was originally commissioned by Napoleon I, and its seventeen stone arches correspond with the seventeen letters that make up the name, Napoleon Bonaparte.

Churches of Bordeaux

The crypt at the Basilique Saint Seurin dates back to the 4th century. The throne features fine woodcarving and was once graced by a pope. It is also a landmark on one of the paths associated with Saint Jacques de Compostela. It is located at Triangle/St Pierre Bordeaux and can be viewed free of charge. Built in the 1400s, Basilique Saint Michel at Place Meynard is considerably more recent. It is however noteworthy for other reasons. Its spire is 121.9m high, making it one of the highest of southwestern France. Here, panoramic views of the surrounding landscape can be admired. Basilique Saint Michel was built in Gothic style and features a dramatic depiction of Saint Michael slaying a dragon at the pulpit.

Although Cathédrale St-André dates back to 1096, when it was consecrated by Pope Urban II, only a single nave wall remains of the original Romanesque features. In 1137, Eleanor of Aquitaine married Louis VII here. Most of its current Gothic facade dates back to the 14th or 15th century. From the top of its belfry, Tour Pey-Berland, you can get a great view of the city. The tower is named after Pey Berland, 15th century archbishop of Bordeaux. Admission is €5.

Jardin Botanique de Bordeaux

The plans for a medicinal garden to be created within Bordeaux had existed since 1629, but this only became a reality almost one hundred years later. During the mid-1880s, this was in turn transformed to something resembling the botanical garden of today. The herbarium now houses around 85,000 specimens and over 3000 plant species are represented in the botanical garden. These include indigenous plants from the province of Aquitaine as well as exotics acquired from China, Japan and the North American continent. Admission is free.

Parc Majorlan, Blanquefort

Avenue du Général de Gaulle,
33290 Blanquefort, France

Parc Majorlan is located near Blanquefort, north of the city Bordeaux and provides a great setting for strolling, exploring or just picnicking. It was initially commissioned by a wealthy banker, Jean Auguste Piganeau as a Baroque style private garden, according to some legends for a beloved, but ailing daughter.

The most unusual features of the park are some man-made limestone caves dating back to the 1800s, but there are also bridges, canyons and waterfalls, as well as a man-made lake of 4 hectares. The park was first opened to the public in 1984. Blanquefort was once independent of the city of Bordeaux, but it is now regarded as one of its outlying communes.

🌎 Château de la Brède

Avenue du Chateau, 33650 La Brede, France
Tel: +33 (0) 5 56 78 47 72
http://www.chateaulabrede.com/

Charles Louis de Secondat, or rather Baron de Montesquieu served as a member of the Parliament of Bordeaux, but is also remembered as an important political philosopher and an advocate of democracy. His ancestral home, a 14th century feudal castle, is now open to the public. The structure is set in a park and enclosed by a traditional moat. Originally the building was accessed via one of three drawbridges, but in recent years, these have since made way for wooden walkways. The park features a sundial, various ornamental trees and even some wildlife, such as deer. The rooms are elegantly furnished and care has been taken to preserve the historical significance of rooms such as Montesquieu's workspace. Admission for a detailed guided tour is €7. The castle is open from the end of April to October. Do inquire about the starting times of official tours.

🌍 Prehistoric Sites

Located near Montignac in the Dordogne region, the Lascaux caves were first discovered in 1940 by four local teenagers. They contain a large treasure of Cro Magnon art, believed to date back to 17, 300 years ago. Over 2000 figures have been documented. These include depictions of humans, various animals such as horses, bison and mammoths as well as abstract art. The most spectacular example is of a 5.5m bull, rendered with surprising attention to detail.

The caves were open to the public between 1948 and 1963, and visited by more than a million sightseers, but when the paintings began to show signs of deterioration, other plans had to be made. Nowadays, the caves are visited rarely, and only by researchers. A replica of two of the caves, Lascaux II was created at a cost of 500 million francs. Here, under project leader Monique Peytral, twenty artists had worked painstakingly to reproduce some of the paintings using the same materials and techniques. A 40 minute guided tour is conducted in French or English.

Another facility, Le Thot, displays an exhibition featuring photographs from Lascaux and also shows a video on the making Lascaux II. Several of the animals depicted in the cave paintings, such as European bison, aurochs and deer can be seen on the grounds and there is a re-creation of a prehistoric village. Admission to Lascaux II costs €8, but a combination ticket that allows entry to Lascaux II and Le Thot can be bought for €12.50.

🌐 Bay of Arcachon

Dune du Pyla

Located about 60km from the city Bordeaux, at the southern part of the Bay of Arcachon, Dune du Pyla is widely acknowledged to be the highest sand dune in Europe. It is 2.5km long, 500m wide if measured in an east-west direction and reaches the height of 107m. The dune first took shape over 5000 years ago.

Besides Dune du Pyla, there are over 1500 dunes of which over 40 are higher than 70m. The area is popular for surfing and sand surfing. In the early evening, it is possible to watch marine animals such as dolphins and porpoises enjoying the warm waters of the bay. The dune is accessible by train to the Arcachon station and by car via Highway A63. Keep to the

A660 Bassin d'Arcachon Biscarrosse, until you get to Exit D259. The summit of the dune offers great views of the Atlantic Ocean and Landes Forest.

Arcachon Museum & Aquarium

2, rue du Professeur Jolyet, Arcachon 33120
Tel: +33 (0) 5 56 83 33 32

Another attraction located along the Bay of Arcachon is the Arcachon Museum and Aquarium. The facility was founded in 1865 and is one of the oldest aquariums in the world. The museum includes specimens of various sea creatures as well as artefacts of historical and archaeological significance.

The aquarium has 36 tanks in total, displaying molluscs, crustaceans, various types of fish and green turtles. It is also a research station that collaborates on a number of programmes with the University of Marine Biology.

BORDEAUX TRAVEL GUIDE

Recommendations for the Budget Traveller

🌐 Accommodation

Ibis Bordeaux Centre Bastide

16 Allee Serr, Zac Coeur de Bastide, 33100 Bordeaux, France
Tel: +33 (0) 5 57 30 00 90
http://www.ibis.com/gb/hotel-6177-ibis-bordeaux-centre-bastide/index.shtml

The Ibis Bordeaux Centre Bastide is located across the river from most of the city's attractions, but within easy access. Rooms include a flatscreen TV, air conditioning, modern bathroom facilities with hairdryer and free wifi internet coverage. The hotel has a business center and is wheelchair friendly. Rooms are clean and well maintained. Accommodation begins at €67. The Ibis hotel group offers several other accommodation options in and around the city of Bordeaux where you can expect no frills accommodation at affordable rates. There is also a loyalty program that offers special benefits to regulars.

BORDEAUX TRAVEL GUIDE

Hotel Gambetta

66 rue de la porte Dijeaux, 33000 Bordeaux, France

Tel: +33 (0) 5 56 51 21 83

http://www.hotel-gambetta.com/

Hotel Gambetta is located centrally within the city of Bordeaux, near the business and shopping districts. Rooms are spacious, cheerfully decorated, comfortable and well maintained. Reception is manned round the clock. Rooms include a wardrobe and television and there is free wifi coverage throughout the hotel. Accommodation begins at €65. Breakfast is extra, at €7 and €0.85 per day is levied as tourism tax.

Hotel Le Chantry

155 rue Georges Bonnac, 33000 Bordeaux, France

http://citotel-le-chantry.hotel-rez.com/

Hotel Le Chantry is within easy access of the city's attractions and various dining and shopping opportunities. Rooms are clean and well maintained and the hotel's staff can be described as friendly and helpful. Reception is available 24 hours and there is a safe-deposit box at the front. Rooms include television, shower facilities, hairdryer, air-conditioning and free wifi. The hotel is wheelchair friendly. Accommodation begins at €60 per night. A buffet breakfast is served, but this is an optional €9 extra.

Chez Simon

21 Rue St Simon, Blaye
http://www.bordeauxwinelands.com/

If you wish to truly experience the wine lands of Bordeaux up close, you may want to book your accommodation in one of the wine regions instead of in the city. Chez Simon offers fine self-catering apartments that are individually owned and available for rent at the discretion of the owner. It is located in the oldest street of the town of Blaye, right by the ferry.

Each apartment is fully furnished and includes conveniences such as a fridge, oven, washing machine, dishwasher and free wifi at between €73 and €89 per night. There is a video library as well as communal barbeque area. Inquire about availability.

Staying at a Wine Chateau

Château Pierre de Lune
1, Chatelet-Sud, Saint-Emilion 33330
Tel: +33 (0) 5 57 74 49 72
http://www.chateau-pierredelune.com/

BORDEAUX TRAVEL GUIDE

Château Franc Pourret

Tel: +33 (0) 5 57 24 72 29

http://www.ouzoulias-vins.com/uk/index.html

Château Monlot Capet

Saint-Hippolyte, 33330

Tel: +33 (0) 5 57 74 49 47

http://www.chateaumonlot.com/

Château Grande Maye

Rouye, 33350 Belves-de-Castillon

Tel: +33 (0) 5 57 47 93 92

Château Terrasson

Château Terrasson, 33570 Puisseguin

Tel: +33 (0) 5 57 56 06 65

http://www.chateau-terrasson.com/frame_uk.htm

The best way to truly soak up the atmosphere of a Bordeaux wine chateau is to stay on one. There are a number of chateaux in Bordeaux that have made a limited number of rooms available for guests. Often wine tasting and a personalized tour with your host is included in the price. Château Pierre de Lune has four rooms and charges between €60 and €80 per night for bed and breakfast. Château Franc Pourret has two double rooms available and charge €109 per night, including breakfast. There is a slight discount, if you are planning a stay of longer than four nights.

Château Monlot Capet has five rooms available and accommodation begins at €80 per night for bed and breakfast. At Château Grande Maye, three double rooms are available. One has a private bathroom, while the other two share bathroom facilities. Accommodation costs between €45 and €50 for bed and breakfast. Château Terrasson offers a self-catering apartment where accommodation costs between €60 and €80 per room per night.

Places to Eat

Le Parlement des Graves

9, Rue du Parlement Sainte-Catherine, 33000 Bordeaux, France
Tel: +33 (0) 5 56 51 68 54
http://www.leparlementdesgraves.fr/

Le Parlement des Graves is centrally located near Place de la Bourse and offers some great combinations of starters, mains and desserts. Some of the aperitifs include salmon carpaccio and the warm goat's cheese and walnut starter, while main dishes offer choices that include lamb, beef and duck. Favorites include the pork tenderloin in honey with caramelised onion and the rack of lamb. You will probably round off the meal with a delectable dessert such as crème brulee, apple crumble or 'ile flottante' - caramelised meringue served with custard sauce. A three-course meal cost you around €24.50 to €26, but remember that wine will be charged separately.

Vinset

27 rue des Bahutiers, 33000 Bordeaux, France
http://www.vinset.fr/

If you are slightly intimidated by the overwhelming variety of wines available in Bordeaux and could do with a little guidance, visit one of the city's wine bars. Vinset offers one of the largest selections of wine, but if you simply state your preferences, your friendly and knowledgeable host should be able to match you to a vintage that matches your taste. To comply with French laws, Vinset also offers a range of local produce, such as cheeses, foie gras, cold meats and from the desserts, authentic St Emilion macaroons with raspberry jam to accompany your wine. The cold meats platter is only €3. Expect to pay between €3 and €7 per glass for the wine. If you love what you drank, Vinset also offers the opportunity to buy wines at cellar prices.

BORDEAUX TRAVEL GUIDE

Lard et Bouchon

22 rue Guadet, 33330 Saint-Emilion, France
Tel: +33 (0) 5 57 24 28 53
http://www.lardetbouchon.fr/

Lard et Bouchon in Saint-Emilion features an interesting interior, made to resemble a wine cave. The menu varies on a day-to-day basis, but some of the favorites you could hope to encounter, includes duck, foie gras and a crab and avocado starter. A dessert highlight is the cafe gourmand, which features a selection of different dessert treats. The price structure is fairly simple. For lunch, a meal consisting of a starter, main dish and dessert will cost €18. For dinner, expect to pay €28 for a starter, main dish and dessert.

Le Petit Port

3 Cours du Port, Blaye, France
Tel: +33 (0) 5 57 42 99 95

Enjoy the leisurely pace of Blaye while dining at this friendly sidewalk cafe. The menu includes dishes such as veal in cream sauce, duck, seafood salad, goat's cheese salad, foie gras, monkfish casserole and fresh fish. Some of the dessert favorites are canelé - a Bordeaux speciality and chocolate mousse. Expect to pay between €15 and €30.

Chai Pascal

37, Rue Guadet, 33330 Saint-Emilion, France

Tel: +33 (0) 5 57 24 52 45

http://www.chai-pascal.com/

Do not let yourself be fooled by the deceptive simplicity of Chai Pascal's menu. This attractive restaurant has a number of tasty surprises, such as the duck, the apple pie and the fish of the day. Other menu items include rabbit with vegetables, lentil soup and goat's cheese salad. Service is friendly and portions are well presented. Most main dishes are priced between €10 and €15 and the free wifi coverage is an added bonus.

Shopping

How To Buy Affordable Wine in Bordeaux

When visiting Bordeaux, you will no doubt be looking to buy some wine to take home with you. The good news is, that there are certain strategies to follow to make your wine purchases without completely breaking your budget. While the top range wines attract a lot of attention, a large percentage of wines from

BORDEAUX TRAVEL GUIDE

the region can be bought for under $20. The question is, how do you know which of the more affordable wines, can be expected to yield good quality.

One tip, from several experts is to look for a slightly higher alcohol content, something in the region of 13 to 13.8 percent. There is solid reasoning behind this. Most Bordeaux reds are blended from cabernet sauvignon and merlot grapes. The richness of flavor to be found in a wine is often directly related to the ripeness of the merlot grapes that went into the mix. Riper grapes also mean higher alcohol content. A second clue, that also hides in the label of the wine, are the words "Mis En Bouteille au Château", which means that the wine was bottled at the winery. Select wine from a great vintage year.

Another tip is to buy from those regions neighboring the top end Bordeaux wine estates. Here you can often find great value for money. For example, Moulis-en-Médoc is within close proximity of the more famous Saint Julien, Saint-Estèphe and Margaux. Côtes de Castillon lies near Saint Émilion. Lalande de Pomerol and Fronsac are located near the prestigious Chateau de Pétrus.

If you are unable to make up your mind within the close proximity of the wine region, why not visit Bordeaux Magnum (http://www.bordeaux-magnum.com/) at 3, Rue Gobineau, a wine shop within the capital that stocks 1500 different wines at affordable prices. Another wine shop is Bordeaux Provenance, which is located at 2 Cours du 30 Juillet.

Cadiot-Badie

26 Allées Tourny, Bordeaux, Bordeaux Centre, 33000
Tel: +33 (0) 5 56 52 23 72
http://cadiot-badie.com/

Cadiot-Badie has a long history, going back to 1860 and the decor is a feast for the eye. Its chocolate candies and other delicious treats should prove irresistible to anyone with a sweet tooth. Expect to find truffles, pralines, liqueurs and also candied fruits. Novelty items that should delight as gifts are the chocolate shaped mini-Eiffel towers.

Les Douceurs de Louise

Address: Les Douceurs de Louise, 10 Place des Grands Hommes, Bordeaux City, 33000
Tel: +33 (0) 5 56 48 14 45

Another great stop for food lovers is Les Douceurs de Louise, an authentic French patisserie shop. The owner Philippe

Andrieu draws inspiration from a variety of flavors to create pastries, chocolate treats and other delicacies.

Rue Saint Catherine

At 1.2km, this is the longest pedestrianized shopping street in Europe and is one of two main arteries that pass through the historical section of the city Bordeaux. It includes the opulent shopping arcade, Gallerie Bordelaise, which dates back to 1830 and a number of more exclusive shops on the Grand Theatre side, as well as Galleries Lafayette, at number 16, which has outlets for a number of well-known fashion brands such as Prada, Hugo Boss, Versace, DKNY and Armani. Galleries Lafayette also has a bookshop, Mollat, which has a large number of English titles. Rue Saint Catherine extends from Place de la Victorie to the Grand Theatre. Mind your step when it's raining, as the tiles can get quite slippery when wet.

La Mauvaise Réputation

19 rue des Argentiers, 33000 Bordeaux
Tel: 05 56 79 73 54

What is it about France that brings out something a little risque and naughty in most people? La Mauvaise Réputation is a bookshop centered around a specific theme. It features books

BORDEAUX TRAVEL GUIDE

and art associated with a bad reputation or some type of taboo. It includes books on body art, such as tattoos and piercing, graphic novels, eroticism and sex. If you are easily shocked, you should perhaps give this one a miss.

BORDEAUX TRAVEL GUIDE

Know Before You Go

🌐 Entry Requirements

By virtue of the Schengen agreement, visitors from other countries in the European Union will not need a visa when visiting France. Additionally Swiss visitors are also exempt. Visitors from certain other countries such as Andorra, Canada, the United Kingdom, Ireland, the Bahamas, Australia, the USA, Chile, Costa Rica, Croatia, El Salvador, Guatemala, Honduras, Israel, Malaysia, Mauritius, Monaco, Nicaragua, New Zealand, Panama, Paraguay, Saint Kitts and Nevis, San Marino, the Holy See, Seychelles, Taiwan and Japan do not need visas for a stay of less than 90 days. Visitors to France must be in possession of a valid passport that expires no sooner than three months after the intended stay. UK citizens will not need a visa to enter France. Visitors must provide proof of residence, financial support and the reason for their visit. If you wish to work or study in France, however, you will need a visa.

🌐 Health Insurance

Citizens of other EU countries are covered for emergency health care in France. UK residents, as well as visitors from Switzerland are covered by the European Health Insurance Card (EHIC), which can be applied for free of charge. Visitors from non-Schengen countries will need to show proof of private health insurance that is valid for the duration of their stay in France (that offers at least €37,500 coverage), as part of their visa application. A letter of coverage will need to be submitted to the French Embassy along with your visa application. American travellers will need to check whether their regular medical insurance covers international travel. No special vaccinations are required.

🌐 Travelling with Pets

France participates in the Pet Travel Scheme (PETS) which allows UK residents to travel with their pets without requiring quarantine upon re-entry. Certain conditions will need to be met. The animal will have to be microchipped and up to date on rabies vaccinations. In the case of dogs, France also requires vaccination against distemper. If travelling from another EU member country, you will need an EU pet passport. Regardless of the country, a Declaration of Non-Commercial Transport must be signed stating that you do not intend to sell your pet.

BORDEAUX TRAVEL GUIDE

A popular form of travel with pets between the UK and France is via the Eurotunnel, which has special facilities for owners travelling with pets. This includes dedicated pet exercise areas and complimentary dog waste bags. Transport of a pet via this medium costs €24. The Calais Terminal has a special Pet Reception Building. Pets travelling from the USA will need to be at least 12 weeks old and up to date on rabies vaccinations. Microchipping or some form of identification tattoo will also be required. If travelling from another country, do inquire about the specific entry requirements for your pet into France and also about re-entry requirements in your own country.

🌍 Airports

There are three airports near Paris where most international visitors arrive. The largest of these is **Charles De Gaulle** (CDG) airport, which serves as an important hub for both international and domestic carriers. It is located about 30km outside Paris and is well-connected to the city's rail network. Most trans-Atlantic flights arrive here. **Orly** (ORY) is the second largest and oldest airport serving Paris. It is located 18km south of the city and is connected to several public transport options including a bus service, shuttle service and Metro rail. Most of its arrivals and departures are to other destinations within Europe. **Aéroport de Paris-Beauvais-Tillé** (BVA), which lies in Tillé near Beauvais, about 80km outside

BORDEAUX TRAVEL GUIDE

Paris, is primarily used by Ryanair for its flights connecting Paris to Dublin, Shannon Glasgow and other cities.

There are several important regional airports. **Aéroport Nice Côte d'Azur** (NCE) is the 3rd busiest airport in France and serves as a gateway to the popular French Riviera. **Aéroport Lyon Saint-Exupéry** (LYS) lies 20km east of Lyon and serves as the main hub for connections to the French Alps and Provence. It is the 4th busiest airport of France. **Aéroport de Bordeaux** (BOD) served the region of Bordeaux. **Aéroport de Toulouse – Blagnac** (TLS), which lies 7km from Toulouse, provides access to the south-western part of France. **Aéroport de Strasbourg** (SXB), which lies 10km west of Strasbourg, served as a connection to Orly, Paris and Nice. **Aéroport de Marseille Provence** (MRS) is located in the town of Marignane, about 27km from Marseille and provides access to Provence and the French Riviera. **Aéroport Nantes Atlantique** (NTE) lies in Bouguenais, 8km from Nantes carriers and provides a gateway to the regions of Normandy and Brittany in the western part of France. **Aéroport de Lille** (LIL) is located near Lesquin and provides connections to the northern part of France.

🌐 Airlines

Air France is the national flag carrier of France and in 2003, it merged with KLM. The airline has a Flying Blue rewards

BORDEAUX TRAVEL GUIDE

program, which allows members to earn, accumulate and redeem Flying Blue Miles on any flights with Air France, KLM or any other Sky Team airline. This includes Aeroflot, Aerolineas Argentinas, AeroMexico, Air Europa, Alitalia, China Airlines, China Eastern, China Southern, Czech Airlines, Delta, Garuda Indonesia, Kenya Airways, Korean Air, Middle Eastern Airlines, Saudia, Tarom, Vietnam Airlines and Xiamen Airlines.

Air France operates several subsidiaries, including the low-cost Transavia.com France, Cityjet and Hop! It is also in partnership with Air Corsica. Other French airlines are Corsairfly and XL Airways France (formerly Star Airlines).

France's largest intercontinental airport, Charles de Gaulle serves as a hub for Air France, as well as its regional subsidiary, HOP!. It also functions as a European hub for Delta Airlines. Orly Airport, also in Paris, serves as the main hub for Air France's low cost subsidiary, Transavia, with 40 different destinations, including London, Madrid, Copenhagen, Moscow, Casablanca, Algiers, Amsterdam, Istanbul, Venice, Rome, Berlin and Athens. Aéroport de Marseille Provence (MRS) outside Marseille serves as a hub to the region for budget airlines such as EasyJet and Ryanair. Aéroport Nantes Atlantique serves as a French base for the Spanish budget airline, Volotea.

BORDEAUX TRAVEL GUIDE

🌐 Currency

France's currency is the Euro. It is issued in notes in denominations of €500, €200, €100, €50, €20, €10 and €5. Coins are issued in €2, €1, 50c, 20c, 10c, 5c, 2c and 1c.

🌐 Banking & ATMs

If your ATM card is compatible with the MasterCard/Cirrus or Visa/Plus networks and configured for a 4-digit PIN, you will have no problem drawing money in France. Most French ATMs have an English language option. Remember to inform your bank of your travel plans before you leave. Keep an eye open around French ATMs to avoid pickpockets or scammers.

🌐 Credit Cards

Credit cards are frequently used throughout France, not just in shops, but also to pay for metro tickets, parking tickets, and motorway tolls and even to make phone calls at phone booths. MasterCard and Visa are accepted by most vendors. American Express and Diners Club are also accepted by the more tourist oriented businesses. Credit cards issued in Europe are smart cards that that are fitted with a microchip and require a PIN for each transaction. This means that a few ticket machines, self-service vendors and other businesses may not be configured to accept the older magnetic strip credit cards.

🌐 Tourist Taxes

All visitors to France pay a compulsory city tax or tourist tax ("taxe de séjour"), which is payable at your accommodation. Children are exempt from tourist tax. The rate depends on the standard of accommodation, starting with €0.75 per night for cheaper establishments going up to €4, for the priciest options. Rates are, of course, subject to change.

🌐 Reclaiming VAT

If you are not from the European Union, you can claim back VAT (or Value Added Tax) paid on your purchases in France. The VAT rate in France is 20 percent on most goods, but restaurant goods, food, transport and medicine are charged at lower rates. VAT can be claimed back on purchases of over €175 from the same shop, provided that your stay in France does not exceed six months. Look for shops that display a "Tax Free" sign. The shop assistant must fill out a form for reclaiming VAT. When you submit it at the airport, you can expect your refund to be debited within 30 to 90 days to your credit card or bank account. It can also be sent by cheque.

BORDEAUX TRAVEL GUIDE

🌐 Tipping Policy

In French restaurants, a 15 percent service charge is added directly to your bill and itemized with the words *service compris* or "tip included". This is a legal requirement for taxation purposes. If the service was unusually good, a little extra will be appreciated. In an expensive restaurant where there is a coat check, you may add €1 per coat. In a few other situations, a tip will be appreciated. You can give an usherette in a theatre 50 cents to €1, give a porter €1 per bag for helping with your luggage or show your appreciation for a taxi driver with 5-10 percent over the fare. It is also customary to tip a hair dresser or a tour guide 10 percent.

🌐 Mobile Phones

Most EU countries, including France uses the GSM mobile service. This means that most UK phones and some US and Canadian phones and mobile devices will work in France. While you could check with your service provider about coverage before you leave, using your own service in roaming mode will involve additional costs. The alternative is to purchase a French SIM card to use during your stay in France. France has four mobile networks. They are Orange, SFR, Bouygues Telecom and Free. In France, foreigners are barred from applying for regular phone contract and the data rates are

BORDEAUX TRAVEL GUIDE

somewhat pricier on pre-paid phone services than in most European countries. You will need to show some form of identification, such as a passport when you make your purchase and it can take up to 48 hours to activate a French SIM card. If there is an Orange Boutique nearby, you can buy a SIM for €3.90. Otherwise, the Orange Holiday package is available for €39.99. Orange also sells a 4G device which enables your own portable Wi-Fi hotspot for €54.90. SFR offers a SIM card, simply known as le card for €9.99. Data rates begin at €5 for 20Mb.

Dialling Code

The international dialling code for France is +33.

Emergency Numbers

All emergencies: (by mobile) 112
Police: 17
Medical Assistance: 15
Fire and Accidents: 18
SOS All Emergencies (hearing assisted: 114)
Visa: 0800 90 11 79
MasterCard: 0800 90 13 87
American Express: 0800 83 28 20

Public Holidays

1 January: New Year's Day (Nouvel an / Jour de l'an / Premier de l'an)

BORDEAUX TRAVEL GUIDE

March - April: Easter Monday (Lundi de Pâques)

1 May: Labor Day (Fête du Travail / Fête des Travailleurs)

8 May: Victory in Europe Day (Fête de la Victoire)

May: Ascension Day (Ascension)

May: Whit Monday (Lundi de Pentecôte)

14 July: Bastille Day (Fête nationale)

15 August: Assumption of Mary (L'Assomption de Marie)

1 November: All Saints Day (La Toussaint)

11 November: Armistace Day (Armistice de 1918)

25 December: Christmas Day (Noël)

Good Friday and St Stephens Day (26 December) are observed only in Alsace and Moselle.

Time Zone

France falls in the Central European Time Zone. This can be calculated as Greenwich Mean Time/Co-ordinated Universal Time (GMT/UTC) +2; Eastern Standard Time (North America) -6; Pacific Standard Time (North America) -9.

Daylight Savings Time

Clocks are set forward one hour on the last Sunday of March and set back one hour on the last Sunday of October for Daylight Savings Time.

BORDEAUX TRAVEL GUIDE

🌐 School Holidays

The academic year in France is from the beginning of September to the end of June. The long summer holiday is from the beginning of July to the end of August. There are three shorter vacation periods. All schools break up for a two week break around Christmas and New Year. There are also two week breaks in February and April, but this varies per region, as French schools are divided into three zones, which take their winter and spring vacations at different times.

🌐 Driving Laws

The French drive on the ride hand side of the road. If you have a non-European driving licence, you will be able to use it in France, provided that the licence is valid and was issued in your country of residence before the date of your visa application. There are a few other provisions. The minimum driving age in France is 18. Your licence will need to be in French or alternately, you must carry a French translation of your driving permit with you.

In France, the speed limit depends on weather conditions. In dry weather, the speed limit is 130km per hour for highways, 110km per hour for 4-lane expressways and 90km per hour for 2 or 3-lane rural roads. In rainy weather, this is reduced to 110km, 100km and 80km per hour respectively. In foggy weather with poor visibility, the speed limit is 50km per hour on all roads. On urban roads, the speed limit is also 50km per hour.

By law, French drivers are obliged to carry a breathalyser in their vehicle, but these are available from most supermarkets, chemists and garages for €1. The legal limit is 0.05, but for new drivers who have had their licence for less than three years, it is 0.02. French motorways are called autorouts. It is illegal in France to use a mobile phone while driving, even if you have a headset.

🌐 Drinking Laws

The legal drinking age in France is 18. The drinking policy regarding public spaces will seem confusing to outsiders. Each municipal area imposes its own laws. In Paris, alcohol consumption is only permitted in licensed establishments. It is strictly forbidden in parks and public gardens.

🌐 Smoking Laws

From 2007, smoking has been banned in indoor spaces such as schools, government buildings, airports, offices and factories in France. The ban was extended in 2008 to hospitality venues such as restaurants, bars, cafes and casinos. French trains have been smoke free since December 2004.

Electricity

Electricity: 220-240 volts

Frequency: 50 Hz

Electricity sockets in France are unlike those of any other country. They are hermaphroditic, meaning that they come equipped with both prongs and indents. When visiting from the UK, Ireland, the USA or even another European country, you will need a special type of adaptor to accommodate this. If travelling from the USA, you will also need a converter or step-down transformer to convert the current to to 110 volts, to avoid damage to your appliances. The latest models of many laptops, camcorders, mobile phones and digital cameras are dual-voltage with a built in converter.

Food & Drink

France is a paradise for dedicated food lovers and the country has a vast variety of well-known signature dishes. These include foie gras, bouillabaisse, escargots de Bourgogne, Coq au vin, Bœuf Bourguignon, quiche Lorraine and ratatouille. A great budget option is crêpes or pancakes. Favorite sweets and pastries include éclairs, macarons, mille-feuilles, crème brûlée and croissants.

The country is home to several world-famous wine-growing regions, including Alsace, Bordeaux, Bourgogne, Champagne,

BORDEAUX TRAVEL GUIDE

Corse, Côtes du Rhône, Languedoc-Roussillon, Loire, Provence and Sud-Ouest and correctly matching food to complimentary wine choices is practically a science. Therein lies the key to enjoying wine as the French do. It accompanies the meal. Drinking wine when it is not lunch or dinner time is sure to mark you as a foreigner. Pastis and dry vermouth are popular aperitifs and favorite after-dinner digestifs include cognac, Armagnac, calvados and eaux de vie. The most popular French beer is Kronenbourg, which originates from a brewery that dates back to 1664.

Websites

http://www.rendezvousenfrance.com/
http://www.france.com/
http://www.francethisway.com/
http://www.france-voyage.com/en/
http://www.francewanderer.com/
http://wikitravel.org/en/France
http://www.bonjourlafrance.com/index.aspx

Printed in Great Britain
by Amazon